KITTEN PACK

THE
KITTEN
HANDBOOK

CLAIRE ARROWSMITH
B.Sc. (Hons), M.Sc.

BOWTIE PRESS®
www.bowtiepress.com

First published in the USA and Canada
by BowTie Press
A Division of BowTie, Inc.
3 Burroughs
Irvine, CA 92618
www.bowtiepress.com

Library of Congress
Cataloging-in-Publication Data

Arrowsmith, Claire.
  The kitten pack : making the most of
kitty's first year / by Claire
Arrowsmith.
    p. cm.
  Includes index.
  ISBN 978-1-933958-69-9
  1. Kittens--Handbooks, manuals, etc. I.
Title.

SF447.A77 2009
636.8--dc22

2009004060

The Author

Claire Arrowsmith was raised in the Highlands of Scotland with a range of domestic, farm, and wild animals that fueled her love of and interest in all animals, particularly cats and dogs. Claire is a full member of the Association of Pet Behaviour Counsellors (APBC) and runs her own behavioral consultancy. She holds an Honours degree in Zoology and a Masters degree in Applied Animal Behaviour and Animal Welfare. Claire has worked in animal rescue and with Hearing Dogs for Deaf People. She is also the specialist behaviorist for Houndstar Films, which produces cat, dog, and small animal advisory DVDs.

She is the author of *What If My Cat?* (with Francesca Riccomini) and *The Sit, Down, Come, Heel, Stay and Stand Book*. She currently lives in England with her husband, Ross, their kitten, Pickle, and their Rhodesian Ridgeback mix, Sarnie.

Printed in China
through Printworks Int Ltd
13 12 11 10 09   1 2 3 4 5

Acknowledgments

I would like to thank the cat breeders who offered such good advice to me during the course of writing this book, and also say thank you to Ruth for reading through the text and for making great suggestions. Your help was greatly appreciated.

The recommendations in this book are given without any guarantees on the part of the author and publisher. If in doubt, seek the advice of a vet or pet-care specialist.

CONTENTS

MY KITTEN'S DETAILS

Kitten's Details

Pet Name..

Pedigree Name ....

Date of Birth ....

Sex.............................. Breed ....

Microchip Number...

Registered Organization ....

My Details

Name..

Address...

Phone...

Breeder's Details

Name..

Address...

Phone...

E-mail...

Registered affix...

Suitable times for contacting ....

Veterinary Clinic's Details

Veterinarian..

Practice Name...

Address...

Phone...

Hours of operation ....

After-hours emergency number...

About My Kitten

My kitten's breed ....

Male/female...

Color ....

Coat type...

Average adult weight will be ....

The breed characteristics are..

I found my kitten via:

❑ An animal shelter

❑ A local ad

❑ Recommendation from my vet or a friend

❑ A cat organization breed list

❑ Meeting a breeder at a cat show

I purchased my kitten from here because:

Checklist for Choosing My Kitten

❑ Does my kitten appear healthy and alert?

❑ Is my kitten confident?

❑ Does my kitten have clean eyes, nose, and ears?

❑ Does my kitten have a clean coat and bottom?

❑ Is my kitten already using a litter box?

❑ Has my kitten passed a health check?

I would like my kitten to be a:　❑ pet only　❑ show cat　❑ breeding cat

Why I wanted a kitten:

Contract and Conditions of Sale

Most breeders will have their own contract, which you should read carefully. An animal shelter will have drawn up formal documents, which you will be required to sign. You can attach these forms here.

Name of kitten..

Registration number/ID......................(CFA) ....(TICA) ....(ACFA) ....(CFF)

Breed...

Sex..

Date of birth:... Sire... Dam................................

---

1 Price of kitten:

2 The owner agrees to take the kitten for a veterinary examination within 3 days of receipt. The breeder will be informed of any problems within this time frame.

3 The breeder guarantees that this kitten is from healthy stock and has had the appropriate vaccinations and parasite control, as stated in the health records.

4 The breeder guarantees the kitten is free from Feline Leukemia (FeLV) and Feline Immuno-deficiency Virus (FIV) at the time of purchase.

5 The owner agrees to inform the breeder of any health problem or abnormality in this kitten as he matures.

6 If the owner wishes to re-home the kitten at any stage in his life, he will inform the breeder, who will offer to buy the kitten/cat back.

7 The kitten should receive regular health checks and annual booster shots as advised by your veterinarian. It is the owner's responsibility to ensure veterinary advice is sought if the kitten shows any signs of illness or distress at any time during his life.

8 If this kitten has been sold as a pet only or is registered as Non-Active, the owner agrees to spay or neuter it by 8 months of age. On receiving proof of neutering, the breeder will forward the registration documents to the owner.

9 Any kittens arising from the breeding of a cat listed as Non-Active or under restriction endorsement will not be eligible for registration.

10 If the kitten has been sold as a breeding cat, the owner agrees to follow recommended guidelines and regulations set by the governing body.

11 The breeder will offer advice about breeding and raising kittens but is in no way responsible for the kittens, for their costs, or for rehoming them.

12 Miscellaneous conditions as appropriate and agreed upon (separate attachment).

Breeder's Signature................................... Date...

Owner's Signature..................................... Date...

Address... Tel no...

The official feline governing bodies will issue formal registration documents for pedigree kittens that fit their criteria. Once completed, this will register you as the owner of the kitten. This documentation will be required should you decide to show your kitten or wish to breed (unless breeding has been banned in your endorsements). You may have to provide proof of health checks or neutering before your breeder releases this paperwork.

If your kitten has no registration documents, you may wish to use this space to insert some photos of your kitten, perhaps with his siblings or the breeder.

7

Pedigree

Although the majority of kittens are wonderful nonpedigree cats, some people choose to acquire a known breed of kitten. Registered kittens can be shown to be genuine specimens of that named breed. A pedigree kitten should come with his own pedigree papers, which show his family tree over at least three generations.

Endorsements

A breeder is entitled to place an endorsement on any pedigree kitten that they sell. This may state that the kitten is not fit for breeding or that the kitten must be shown to pass certain health checks before permission will be granted to allow him to be bred from. The purpose of this is to ensure that the breed standard is maintained and to prevent any inherited problems from being passed on. In these cases your paperwork will probably state that no offspring can be registered or that your kitten is Non-Active. You should be fully aware of any endorsements before you buy the kitten. Most endorsements

left: A pedigree kitten will have a traceable family history and will resemble his relatives.

Don't assume a kitten is pedigree.

above: **Ask if the parent's have passed health checks before purchase.**
left: **Some kittens may not be ideal for showing or breeding.**
right: **A breeder may lift an endorsement.**

affect only those wanting to breed from their kitten, so you must discuss your requirements with the breeder before you sign the contracts.

Pedigree Siamese are popular.

My Kitten's Pedigree Endorsements

Name of owner . . . .

Address of owner . . . .

I understand that the kitten . . . .
has been sold to me with a restricting endorsement on the pedigree, and if s/he produces a litter
of kittens they cannot be registered with any feline organization with a view to show or breed.

I understand that I can/cannot have this endorsement lifted, and it will either remain in place for
the kitten's entire life or will be lifted on completion of the requirements stated.

I understand that this endorsement has been placed on this kitten for the following reasons:

❑   The kitten is not a good example of the breed.
❑   It is the breeder's opinion that offspring from this kitten would not conform to breed
     standards.
❑   The kitten carries an inherited condition that could be passed on or pose problems
     to his/her offspring.
❑   The mother had breeding difficulties that could also affect her offspring.
❑   The breeder has requested that the kitten pass the suggested health tests prior to
     breeding.

Owner's signature. . . . . Date . . . .

Name of breeder . . . .

Address of breeder . . . .

This kitten carries an endorsement, which means that either (i) no offspring will be accepted for
official registration or (ii) registration is only possible if both parents have been certified as being
healthy. In this case, the breeder will lift the restriction on receipt of this proof prior to breeding.
This endorsement is placed in order to improve and maintain the breed's health and
conformation and to ensure that anyone considering breeding a cat does so responsibly.

Breeder's signature . . . . Date . . . .

COLLECTING THE KITTEN

There will be a lot of excitement when you collect your kitten, so use this list to ensure that you have everything you need before you bring the kitten home. Missing paperwork can be hard to track down, and diet and care information are vital in the early days. Some breeders will withhold the registration and pedigree papers until you have neutered your kitten. However, these papers should be present for viewing, and the signed contract should state that you will receive the full paperwork on receipt of evidence from your veterinarian.

Checklist Prior to Taking My Kitten Home
(Check or complete if you have these items)

- ❏ Signed contract of sale
- ❏ Signed endorsement record
- ❏ Pedigree papers
- ❏ Registration papers
- ❏ Kitten's health records
- ❏ Receipt for payment
- ❏ Diet sheet provided
- ❏ Food supply provided
- ❏ Kitten care guide provided

- ❏ Insurance provided

Company:..

Policy no:...

Other equipment provided:

Breeder's signature:...Date:..............................

Owner's signature:..Date:..............................

Breeder's Worming Record

This is to certify that:

Kitten's name: ....

Breed: ....

Date of birth: ....

Has been wormed with:

Name of medication: ....

Date of first worming: ....

Date of second worming: ....

Date of third worming: ....

Date of fourth worming: ....

Next worming treatment is due on: ....

Any adverse effects caused by worming treatment: ....

The new owner has been advised and understands the importance of regular worming with appropriate products.

Breeder's signature: ....Date: ....

Owner's signature: ....Date: ....

Worming Routine

It is important to keep your kitten fully up to date with his worming treatments. Complete the above table to show when your kitten received his worming treatments while with the breeder. This record can be shown to your vet during your kitten's initial health examination. You will then be advised about when the next treatment is due so that you can schedule the next treatment in advance and keep up to date. Future treatments can be noted in the Health Care section (see pages 46–47).

Arranging Collection

Being prepared for the new arrival before your kitten is brought home is very important. Arrange for time off, purchase necessary equipment, and kitten-proof your home (as advised in the Safety at Home section on pages 20–21).

Checklist of Preparations

- Will I be at home enough to help my kitten settle in and to build a bond between us?
- Is there a secure area where my kitten can spend time during the day and sleep at night?
- Is there a suitable position for the litter box?
- Where will my kitten's food and water bowl sit?
- Will I be able to keep my other pets safely separated while my kitten settles in?
- Who will be responsible for cleaning out the litter box?
- Have I obtained all the necessary equipment for my kitten?
- Have I researched local veterinary clinics and have I made provisions for the cost of treatments?

Making Arrangements for Collection

The breeder will discuss with you a mutually convenient date and time for you to collect your kitten. The breeder will be able to tell you early on the approximate date when the kittens will be old enough to leave. As it gets closer to the time, you will be able to make more definite arrangements at a time that is convenient for everyone. Some breeders will put the agreed date and time in writing for you. Prior arrangement will allow the breeder to collate all the appropriate paperwork and equipment for a smooth handover of your kitten. If you are collecting your kitten from an animal shelter, you will have to discuss with the staff what hours they are open for rehoming. Don't be late or miss your appointment in either case, as it is impolite to do so, and in some cases you may even miss out on your preferred kitten.

Preparing for Your Journey

Planning ahead will save you from being late for your appointment to collect your kitten and might even allow you to avoid travelling during peak-time traffic. If you have children, it is best that they don't accompany you on the journey.

Checklist of Basic Items Needed

Item Needed	Where to Locate Item	Obtained
Litter box and litter		
Supply of suitable food		
Food and water bowls		
Cat carrier		
Suitable bed or blanket		
Grooming brush and combs		
Scratching post		

Planning the Journey
Travel time to breeder:
Method of transport:
Time of appointment:
Planned departure time:

Questions I would like to ask the breeder:
(Prepare these in advance so you don't forget during the excitement of collecting your kitten)

It's not fair to expect excited children to remain quiet and calm during your journey home. Being accompanied by an adult friend can be useful, however, to keep an eye on your kitten while you drive, or vice versa. Being organized will save you stress and make the journey less traumatic for your new kitten. Remember to allow time for the breeder to go through the details about your kitten's care. Getting home earlier in the day will allow your kitten the chance to settle into your home, eat, and use the litter box before you go to bed.

Make sure that you fill your car with enough gas to get you home without having to make a stop. If you have a long journey, it makes sense to fill up before you arrive at the breeder's home. Being prepared will mean you will minimize the number of stops on the way home. Do not open the cat carrier during your journey, as your kitten may escape. If there is an emergency and you have to check your kitten, make sure all car doors and windows are closed first. Never leave your kitten unsupervised in your car. Excessively hot or cold temperatures can kill kittens very quickly.

Items to Pack in the Car

For you:
- A map or an in-car satellite navigation system (bring your power charger)
- Breeder's full address
- A mobile phone
- The breeder's telephone number
- Your wallet with the agreed payment
- Glasses for reading all the small print
- Your camera or camcorder to record your kitten with his siblings and mother
- A drink and snacks so you can avoid any detours that will prolong your journey or take you out of your car

For your kitten:
- Your cat carrier lined with newspaper and a blanket
- A small bowl and a bottle of water
- A towel and plastic sheet to place underneath your cat carrier in case your kitten urinates or vomits
- A pheromone spray (obtainable from your vet) for spraying on the cat carrier to reduce the kitten's anxiety levels while he is inside

WHEN KITTEN COMES HOME

Carry the cat carrier carefully into the house without swinging or bumping it. Take it straight to the secure area where your kitten will initially be spending his time. Try to keep everyone calm and quiet, and make sure that other pets are kept away so that your kitten doesn't feel frightened. Let your kitten stay in the carrier for a short time while you settle in after your journey. Then open the carrier door and wait for your kitten to emerge. Encourage him out with a soothing voice and by placing some food in his bowl. Never tip the carrier up on its end to get your kitten out, as this will create more stress than necessary.

Settling In

Allow your kitten to come out and investigate his new environment gradually. It is natural for a kitten to sniff everything he encounters. If he feels comfortable, he will mark the item by rubbing his face against it, leaving his scent behind from the sebaceous glands in his head. You'll probably soon find yourself "face bumped" by your kitten at regular intervals. This is a good sign that he feels happy around you.

Some kittens will require longer than others to settle in. Keep a timid kitten within a particular area of the home until his confidence has risen, then begin to open the door to allow him to explore other rooms within the home. Save meetings with other pets for a time when the kitten seems happier to be around you.

left: Open the cat carrier only after you are safely inside the house.

Establishing Good Routines

Getting things right from the start will make owning your kitten far easier in the long run. Try to follow these recommendations:

- Show your kitten his litter box by gently lifting the kitten and placing him in the box.
- Use calm, steady movements, and be careful of where you step while your kitten is loose.
- If you don't want your kitten on the work surfaces, don't ever leave food or toys on there. As soon as your kitten jumps up, pick him up and place him back on the floor.
- Never smack or scruff your kitten. This will only make him nervous of you.
- Restrict your kitten to a small area of the house initially until he has established good litter box habits and feels more confident.
- Spend time petting and grooming your kitten from day one.
- Cats respond to praise and rewards, so make sure you respond appropriately when your kitten does something you like.

below: **Your kitten will need to be taken to his litter box.**

Organization of Routine and Early Records

The person responsible for feeding my kitten is:

First daily meal:

Second daily meal:

Third daily meal:

Fourth daily meal:

The food and water bowls will be placed:

The location of the litter box is:

Who will clean the litter box?

Rooms my kitten has access to:

My kitten's personality is:

Things I'd like to remember about these first few days:

The First Few Days at Home

Establishing a good routine will help you care for your kitten while he gets used to his new life as part of your household. Decide on areas of the home that he is allowed to explore and regular routines that you would like to establish. It is also important that you talk to other family members and agree what your individual responsibilities are and what you will do jointly. You can all record your observations in this book.

A tiny kitten needs to explore his home.

My Kitten's Routine During the First Weeks at Home

My kitten arrived home at: on:

My kitten's safe area will be:

He will then be allowed to explore:

First meal in his new home was:

My kitten knew to use his litter box by:

My kitten's bed will be:

Places where my kitten prefers to sleep:

My kitten's first toys are:

The first game my kitten played was:

Date of first vet appointment:

Date of first grooming session:

Getting to Know My Kitten

Memorable moments during my kitten's first few weeks:

Teaching My Kitten to Respond to His Name

One of the first lessons for a kitten to learn is how to respond to his own name. This is easy to start, but often owners only partially teach this to their cat and as a result don't always experience the ideal results.

- First, decide on the name of your kitten. If family members use different nicknames for him initially, then he will become confused.
- Use treats and toys to encourage your kitten to approach. Say his name and offer the reward.
- Remember to use tiny, tasty treats to encourage him to come to you.
- Practice saying your kitten's name in an excited voice and then reward him for responding.
- Remember that kittens will become bored of the training if you do too much at any one time, so take a break after a few minutes.
- Your kitten will begin to associate the name you have chosen with the arrival of a rewarding experience; whether that is food, a fun game, or petting and attention.

- Practice calling your kitten from across the room and then giving his dinner or a reward.
- Progress with your training as you give your kitten more freedom by calling him from another room, and make sure he has lots of fun when he arrives.
- Eventually you should be able to call your cat successfully from all around your home.

Your feline is not likely to have a completely reliable response at first, especially if he is snoozing comfortably, but if you practice and make it worth your cat's while to come to you, then he is likely to respond well.

Playing with Your Kitten

It is incredibly important to play with your kitten. Your kitten will have lots of energy and needs to exercise freely to aid his physical development as well as to feel mentally satisfied.

Kittens like to practice games that help them develop their physical abilities, such as pouncing, swiping, and leaping. However, an overexuberant kitten can easily become injured, so make sure that you kitten-proof your rooms first (see pages 20–21).

Cats can seem extremely fickle when it comes to playing with the toys their owners buy for them. However, it's important to remember that a kitten will not respond the way a puppy will. Cats get bored of games much more quickly than dogs do and crave more variation in their activities.

When choosing toys, the following factors are important to remember:
- Texture—toys made from materials that feel and sound different are interesting.
- Size—small toys are very enticing.
- Movement—toys that can be rolled around or wiggled will be exciting.
- Smell—this may be the scent of food or catnip designed to increase interest.

Since novelty is vital in keeping a kitten entertained, pack up two or three shoeboxes of different toys. Take one out at a time and each week swap them with another box. This rotation of toys prolongs a kitten's excitement and interest. Remember that toys don't have to be expensive to provide entertainment, and homemade ones are often perfect. You can add new items to the boxes as your kitten grows. Always remove damaged toys or those that may be swallowed once your kitten has grown larger.

> **Safety Tip**
> Never let your kitten play with elastic bands or small aluminum foil balls, as both can be easily swallowed and can cause internal blockages.

Fun Toy Ideas
- Scrunched-up paper balls
- Plastic balls (Ping-Pong size)
- Balls with bells inside
- Cat track with moving balls (shown above)
- Paper bags (cut through the handles first)
- Catnip-stuffed toys
- Small furry toy mice
- Corks and feathers
- Cardboard tubes
- Kitty kongs (hollow rubber toys) stuffed with food

It can take a kitten time to become interested in a new item, so don't panic if a new toy doesn't result in a playing frenzy. It's healthy for a cat to learn to play both alone and with his owner, so try to leave safe toys out for him to find, and bring out the interactive toys during your daily play times. Leave toys in places where your kitten will find them as he moves about your home. Certain areas lend themselves to some toys better than others do: for example, hanging toys are great from open doorjambs or stair wells, while halls or tiled floors provide space and speed for plastic balls to roll and be chased. Toys that hold a small treat can be especially appealing.

Think about which items you might place in your kitten's boxes:

Box 1	Box 2	Box 3

My kitten's favorite toys include:

My kitten likes playing: alone ☐   with me ☐   both ☐

Game Ideas

A great interactive game for kittens uses a fishing-rod-style toy with feathers or tassels attached. You can make one of these wand toys with a long wire with a feather attached at the end. This will move about enticingly when you weave it in front of the kitten. Laser pens have become very popular toys recently. They shine a bright spot of light, which you can move around the floor in front of the kitten. However, great care must be taken when playing with these. Never shine the light in your kitten's eyes, as this could damage them. This game can also create lots of frustration since the cat never gets to catch the "prey." Aim to overcome this problem by "landing" the light on a favorite toy at the end of the game. Some breeds of cats, particularly some of the Orientals, love a game of fetch with a furry toy. Be imaginative, and you'll find something you both enjoy.

Kittens should not play with wand toys on their own.

Safety at Home

A kitten will be surprisingly fast and agile, so it's important to make sure that your home is safe for him to explore. Before you allow your kitten freedom around your home, check each room for hazards. Look on the floor, on surfaces, and upward to find places where your kitten may climb.

Don't assume an area is safe because there is a short gap to cross. A kitten will be extremely inquisitive and will climb into dark, warm areas and could easily become trapped. For this reason, it can help to fit child-locks on cupboards and *always* check your washing machine and dryer before you start them. Kittens will squeeze through the tiniest spaces, so block off any inviting gaps behind kitchen units or around pipework.

Living Room

- Place well-fitting fire guards to prevent escape up **chimneys**.
- Secure screens on **windows**, especially those in apartments where a fall would be fatal.
- Secure or move **fragile ornaments** since a kitten could easily knock them over and be injured by the shards.
- Use only **nonbreakable ornaments** and secure your Christmas tree to prevent it from toppling over if the kitten tries to climb it.
- Create a mesh or plastic screen enclosure around **balconies** to prevents kittens from falling off.

Office

- Keep **elastic bands** and plastic ties stored away securely in a drawer.
- Put **cell phone** chargers away.
- Unplug **electrical items** and secure **wires**

with cable ties or plastic protectors when not in use to prevent electrocution caused by chewing or clawing.

Kitchen

- Dissuade your kitten from jumping up on surfaces where there may be **sharp knives** or hot items.
- Put away the **ironing board**, as this could be turned into a dangerous climbing frame, and the iron could be pulled down onto the kitten.
- Secure **cupboards** to prevent your kitten climbing in and finding toxic foodstuffs or cleaning products.
- Don't use **disinfectants** containing phenol, as a cat's system cannot eliminate them once ingested. These include products that turn cloudy when mixed up.
- Keep your kitten out of the kitchen while cooking is taking place, as there is a danger of you **tripping** or **spilling hot foods** or of the kitten jumping onto a **hot stove**.

Bathroom

- While running a **bath**, don't leave it unattended.
- The **toilet lid** must be lowered or the bathroom door closed at all times.

> **Safety Tip**
> Grow your own cat grass so that your kitten has a safe alternative to munch.

Common Toxic House Plants *Check which ones you own*

Plant	Poisonous part	Plant	Poisonous part
❏ Aloe vera	all parts	❏ Geranium	all parts
❏ Amaryllis	bulb	❏ Holly	all parts
❏ Anemone	all parts	❏ Hyacinth	bulb
❏ Apple	seeds in large numbers	❏ Ivy	all parts
		❏ Jasmine	all parts
❏ Azalea	all parts	❏ Lily—all species**	all parts
❏ Carnation	flower and leaf	❏ Lily of the Valley	all parts
❏ Castor oil plant	leaves and seeds	❏ Mistletoe	all parts
❏ Christmas cherry	all parts	❏ Monkshood	all parts
❏ Christmas rose	all parts	❏ Oleander	all parts
❏ Chrysanthemum	leaves and stems	❏ Philodendron	all parts
❏ Cyclamen	flowers	❏ Poinsettia	leaves, sap and stem
❏ Dragon tree	leaves		
❏ Dumb cane	leaves, stems, roots	❏ Rubber plant	leaves
❏ Elephant's ear	all parts	❏ Umbrella plant	all parts
❏ Ferns	leaves	*(This is a partial list. Consult the ASPCA Poison Control for a complete list.)*	
❏ Foxglove**	all parts, including water from the vase	** *highly toxic*	

- Lock away any **medication**. Tablets may become playthings and be ingested.

Plants

Kittens may chew on tender plant shoots while they investigate their surroundings. Ingesting a small amount of vegetation is natural. However, many indoor plants are actually toxic to cats and some, such as the Easter lily, can be fatal after only minimal contact with the pollen. A new cat owner should always check which plants they have around the home. Replace any problematic ones with safe varieties or make absolutely sure that they are kept out of reach.

Exploring kittens may chew dangerous plants.

EARLY SOCIALIZING

We are now aware that the early experiences that a kitten has will greatly influence his behavior as an adult. The more pleasant and varied these experiences are, the more likely he is to grow up to be confident and interactive.

Research has shown that if young kittens are handled for between 20 to 30 minutes per day, they will grow up liking human contact and often not wanting to resist grooming or physical examination.

Despite this information, kitten socialization is often forgotten or not made a priority. If you want to show your cat or have a busy home life, it is especially important that your kitten learns to cope with new events. Since many feline behavioral problems are caused by anxiety, a thorough socialization is definitely advised.

Socialization is the term used when we discuss a kitten becoming familiar with people and other animals. It's also often used to refer to the process of getting used to new places, items, sounds, and smells, although the correct term for this is actually *habituation*. Both allow the kitten to grow in confidence in a range of situations.

Meeting Family Members and Friends

Meeting a range of people is very important, although you must take care not to overwhelm your kitten. Introduce new people one at a time, and always ask children to be quietly seated at first. Your kitten will have to get used to all the different voices, movements, smells, and types of people. To help him relax, offer your kitten's favorite treat or game to be played, or tell your guests how he likes to be petted. Arrange meetings in different rooms and outside the home, too. It is important that your kitten becomes familiar with people who are not similar to those in his immediate family. If you are particularly quiet, then it would be good social experience to introduce a louder, more confident personality.

Meeting Other Pets

Early experience with other cats is important for the social development of your kitten. If he grows up without meeting or living with another cat, then he is unlikely to be sociable in the future if you try to introduce one. This is just one more argument for adopting two kittens, if you can. If you plan to breed or show, it is important that your kitten grows up able to tolerate others. Some specialists run Kitten Kindergartens for young cats within a clinic setting. However, these need to be organized carefully, or the kittens will feel stressed. After introducing your other pets (see also *The Owner's Handbook* pages 26–27), if the animals cohabit peacefully, it will be a good experience for your kitten. However, don't assume he will feel happy around a friend's dog just because he lives with one at home. Although you can't predict your kitten's reactions to all the animals he may encounter, the more experience you give early on, the more likely he will be to cope confidently later in his life.

Getting Used to Traveling

If you plan to travel to shows or to take your kitten on vacation with you, it's important that he has a chance to become comfortable with traveling. Even if you intend to take your cat out only when he requires a veterinary examination, you can reduce much of the associated stress by getting your kitten accustomed to the experience. A secure cat carrier where your cat feels safe is essential. Begin by placing your cat within his carrier in the car. If your kitten remains relaxed, drive a short distance before returning home. Traveling in this way without the stress of receiving medical treatment or arriving at a noisy show will help to teach your kitten to relax in your car.

Getting your kitten familiar with this can help reduce the likelihood of future resistance to handling within the clinic. A scared cat can be difficult to examine and treat, so it's best to try to prevent this. Booking

below: **A friendly, bouncy puppy can worry a young kitten.**

Veterinary Staff

There's lots of focus these days on introducing puppies to vet staff, but we often forget about doing similar work with our kittens. Veterinary staff often wear uniforms that will smell of other animals and the products they have been using. your kitten in for a few meetings with the veterinary staff, who can pet him and get him used to simple handling procedures (then a quick game or treat), will be useful.

above: **A cat carrier should be a place where your kitten feels secure.**

left: **Ideally, your kitten should meet your vet during routine health checks to build confidence.**

Socialization Record Chart

You will have to ensure that your kitten gets plenty of experience of each of the events listed until at least 6 months of age. Take things slowly with more timid kittens. Record other experiences you think your kitten should get used to.

Expert Tip

A sound effects CD can be used to expose your kitten to a variety of noises that may otherwise be difficult to arrange regularly.

Event	Experience gained (who kitten met and what they were doing)	Notes about my kitten's response/improvement
Meeting various men		
Meeting various women		
Meeting children of various ages		
Experiencing babies		
Visiting friends' homes (safe areas only)		
Visits to meet veterinary clinic staff		
Visiting the groomer		
Party/social gathering		
Cat show		
Other cats		

Event	Experience gained (who kitten met and what they were doing)	Notes about my kitten's response/improvement
Dogs (take great care)		
Other domestic pets in your home and other homes		
Livestock (if you live near the country)		
Vacuum cleaner		
Washing machines		
Clothes dryers		
Hair dryers		
Noisy children's toys		
Vehicles		
Car travel		
Being left alone		
Being groomed		
Medical examination		

GROOMING AND HYGIENE

Kittens and cats are often excellent at keeping themselves clean. However, get into good habits from the beginning, since trying to get to grips with a tangled coat or with a cat who isn't used to being handled can be very difficult. Longhaired cats should be groomed regularly, and older, obese, or ill cats will need some help to ensure good coat care. And the more thorough your grooming is, the less hair will be shed around your home.

above: **If bathing is necessary, make sure the water is warm and that your kitten feels safe.**

Coat Type

Short	Groom once a week
Medium	Groom 2–3 times a week
Long	Groom every day

Start to Groom Your Kitten

Find a safe place in a well-lit area to groom your kitten. You might prefer doing this on the floor, on a nonslip table, or on your lap. Place a rubber mat or cloth on your table to help your kitten remain steady. Calmly and gently stroke your kitten until she begins to relax. Place one hand on her chest to prevent her from moving away. Use a soft bristle brush or a rubber mitt at first, as the sensation is enjoyable. Praise and offer your kitten a nice treat for tolerating this. Long-haired kittens will require more

time for grooming, and attention will be required under the forearms and under the tail. Brushing through the coat backward can help remove excess dead hair, while sprinkling on a little nonperfumed talcum powder can help loosen up mats. Use pet wet wipes to carefully clean the hair around the eyes and ears.

Bathing

Most kittens will not require bathing. If absolutely necessary, lay a towel on the bottom of the bath or sink, and have warm towels ready nearby. Use a little warm water and a small amount of cat shampoo, and rinse thoroughly. Wrap your kitten in the towel and keep her in a warm room. Make sure she is dry before entering a cool room.

Left: **Pay particular attention to longer hair that may mat easily.**

Checking the Ears

Gently bend the ear backward against the head to allow you to look inside. A healthy ear will be clean and pink. If you see wax or other discharge, then seek veterinary advice, as there may be ear mites or an infection present. Never push cotton swabs inside the ear, as this could damage your kitten's hearing. The external part of the ear can be gently wiped during grooming.

Cutting the Nails

Keep your kitten's claws clipped to reduce any damage to furniture. This will not remove the kitten's need to scratch, so also provide a scratching post. Use small cat nail clippers; never use your own scissors or nail clippers, as they may splinter the nail. Stand behind your kitten, hold her steady, and take hold of one paw. Gently push on a pad until the associated claw is extended. Clip off only the transparent nail tip at a 45-degree angle. Don't cut into the pink area: this is the nail quick, which

above: **Choose a time when your kitten is quiet and relaxed before trying to clip nails. Stay calm and offer quiet praise. Take your time and carefully clip just the tip of each claw.**

contains the nerves and blood vessels. Cutting this area will be painful and will cause bleeding. Nail clipping in cats involves the regular removal of a tiny portion at the tip of the claw. For ease, you can just do a couple of nails each time. Your veterinary staff can show you how to do this if you are unsure.

Grooming Equipment

	Short coat	Medium coat	Long coat
Fine-toothed comb	✔		
Wide-toothed comb		✔	✔
Rubber mitt	✔	✔	
Talcum powder		✔	✔
Bristle brush	✔	✔	✔
Nail clippers	✔	✔	✔
Wet wipes	✔	✔	✔
Flea comb	✔	✔	✔

BEHAVIOR ISSUES

Your kitten arrives in your home already influenced by the experiences of her early weeks and by her own genetic makeup. Although cats have lived with humans for thousands of years, they have retained a remarkable similarity to their wild cousins.

Sometimes, their natural instincts or inherited characteristics will create problems while they settle in to life as your pet. Addressing these issues quickly will give you the best chance to solve them completely.

dislike of the box, health problems, or inherited tendencies. You must address this problem quickly. Most kittens learn by observing their mother using her box. If your kitten missed this opportunity, then make sure that you gently put the kitten into the tray after every meal and when she wakes up. Most kittens will then naturally do their business there and learn the correct association.

Bathroom Problems

Although most kittens will arrive in your home with an understanding of what a litter box is for, some will begin to urinate in undesirable places. There are several reasons for this, including

My Kitten's Litter Box

Try to ensure that you can answer yes to all the questions below.		
Is the litter box type familiar to my kitten?	☐ Yes	☐ No
Is it easy for a kitten to climb into?	☐ Yes	☐ No
Am I using a type of litter my kitten recognizes?	☐ Yes	☐ No
Can my kitten find the litter box quickly?	☐ Yes	☐ No
Is it in a quiet place?	☐ Yes	☐ No
Is it away from her food and water bowls?	☐ Yes	☐ No
Is the litter box used only by my kitten, not other cats?	☐ Yes	☐ No
Am I scooping out and cleaning it at least every day?	☐ Yes	☐ No
Does my kitten seem relaxed about using the litter box?	☐ Yes	☐ No

Expert Tip
Never strike your kitten for making any mistake. You'll only make her frightened of you, which will lead to more severe problems.

Some kittens find their litter box difficult to use and seek alternative bathroom places. Complete the questions in the table to help you discover what the problem might be. Refer also to Litter Box Habits in the The Owner's Handbook pages 30–3, and never:

- smack or shake your kitten if she has a bathroom accident.
- rub her nose in any mess she has made.
- force your kitten outside after a bathroom accident.
- change litter type suddenly, as your kitten may not recognize it.
- try to medicate your kitten while she's using the litter box.

above: **An excited kitten can damage curtains or carpets while she practices scratching.**

Scratching Furnishings

Scratching is a behavior all cats perform. Your kitten is learning about which items in her environment are good for scratching, so it's key that you provide enough scratching posts *(left)*. Place a post next to where she has been scratching. Spraying catnip on the post may attract older kittens and adult cats, but you can also entice tiny kittens to pounce and jump on the post by using a cat wand. Praise her for using the post. If you spot your kitten about to scratch your furniture, interrupt with a clap and gently take it to her post. Establish good habits now.

Damaging Furniture When Excited

A kitten's playful nature may be directed toward anything within your home. Many owners find their kitten using their furniture or curtains as playthings. Make sure there are plenty of appropriate toys available, and encourage your kitten to play with these. Place scratching posts and cat towers in her area, and encourage her to jump or scratch on these. A kitten can become frustrated if the toy she is playing with rolls under your sofa, and she may catch her claws while trying to paw it out. Block off these spaces if you don't want to be persistently fetching the toy out.

During "mad" moments, extra energy is burned off.

Play Biting and Scratching

The wrong kind of games will very quickly teach your kitten to play too roughly with you. *Never let your kitten play with your hands or feet.* This may be entertaining with a tiny kitten, but it will quickly become painful and dangerous as she grows larger

and stronger. If your kitten tries to grab or bite you, immediately stop the game. She needs to learn that this means the end of the fun. Later, encourage her attention back onto a toy.

left: **A kitten's play-biting stage should never be encouraged.**

Disliking Being Held

Getting your kitten used to being held is important, and doing this early on will make problems less likely. Practice often and make sure your kitten is supported under her bottom and by her chest. Be calm and quiet and avoid rapid movements. Begin by holding your kitten on your lap or on the floor rather than lifting her into the air. When your kitten relaxes, release her again. If your kitten continues to react badly, make sure there's no reason why she should be feeling pain when being lifted. Also make sure that your kitten is comfortable being near you and with normal stroking all over her body. Don't allow young children to lift your kitten by her limbs or without supporting her properly, as this may make her wary of such contact.

Fearful Behavior

Many kittens will appear frightened at first. After all, they have experienced lots of sudden change in their short lives. However, some kittens are less able to find their confidence. This may be for genetic reasons or because the kitten was not socialized properly. It will be your job to gently teach your kitten to feel safe and secure. The key is to take your time and to not force your kitten to face scary events until she is ready to do so. You must make the situation as comfortable for her as possible. This may mean having strict rules about how your children behave near your kitten, keeping your family dog away, and perhaps even training the dog to behave more appropriately when they do meet. Your kitten should have safe areas where she can hide away and watch the world go by. When she comes out, be quiet, offer tasty morsels, and try to trigger play behavior with a feather or tassel on a string. Do not expect too much all at once. If your kitten is very quiet, it is worth asking your vet to examine her again in case she is feeling ill. Sometimes, a very timid kitten is not right for a busy home. In such cases, it may be kinder to place the kitten in a quieter home.

Lack of Interest in Food

If your kitten started off eating and drinking well and has suddenly changed her habits, then your vet should examine her to rule out any health issues. The stress resulting from being taken from her mother and littermates can often cause a kitten

below: **Make meetings between pets as safe and calm as possible.**

to feel less hungry, but it is vital that she doesn't go without food for over 24 hours. Make sure to serve food that she is used to, and provide a wide and shallow bowl so she can eat without bumping her whiskers against the sides.

If your kitten is not finishing all of her meal but is growing well and looks healthy, then it may be that too much food is being offered and more regular, smaller meals are preferred. Remember that a kitten's stomach is tiny, and cats are not designed to eat large quantities. If your kitten is nervous of people, then she may find eating in front of you too much. Make sure she feels safe and secure by giving her space while eating, and slowly begin to build up her positive associations and confidence in you at other times.

Lack of Interest in Water

Cats were originally desert animals and so naturally get most of their water from their diet. If you are feeding a good-quality canned food, your kitten is probably getting most of her water from that source. Some cats dislike the taste of our tap water, so filtering the water first can help. Others prefer running water and will enjoy a cat water fountain. Your kitten may be finding somewhere else to drink, such as dripping taps or plant pots. These sources may not be safe, so make sure that your kitten feels comfortable about using her water bowl. Placing several bowls around the house will provide a convenient drink whenever your kitten feels the need.

below: **Fresh water is far more enticing than stale water in a bowl, so replace liquid daily.**

BASIC TRAINING

Taking time to try to teach your kitten new actions or a different game will help strengthen the bond between you. Your kitten will associate you with the pleasant social experience and with the petting and rewards that you offer. Her desire to be with you and to interact with you will grow with this experience, so irrespective of whether you aim to teach fancy tricks or just a new game, spending time with your kitten is the best way to build a strong relationship.

How a Kitten Learns

Your kitten knows what she likes and doesn't like and wants to make decisions that will ensure she gets more of the nice things. Training your kitten is about encouraging her to do specific actions to gain the reward. You may try luring your kitten to jump, stretch, or touch using a cat wand or a treat. Training your kitten will take patience, but it's worthwhile as you can make her easier to live with as well as teach some fun actions.

- Your kitten will make fastest progress if you begin training in an area where she feels safe and without many distractions.
- Kitten training should be done in very short sessions with lots of breaks for play and rest.
- Use small amounts of tasty treats.

- Choose actions that come naturally to your kitten.
- Kittens and cats won't continue working with you if you fail to reward them.
- Punishment will put your kitten off training and may damage your relationship.

Your kitten is constantly learning about her world, so it's important that you respond correctly to her actions. If you give her attention for meowing or pouncing on you, then it's likely that these behaviors will occur again.

Using Rewards

All felines, particularly the lazier types, will need a good reason to direct their focus onto training. Choosing a reward that your kitten adores will tempt her to participate in your training exercises for longer. Each cat will differ, so you will have to spend some time finding out what your kitten loves most—a treat, toy, or petting. Remember that cats like variation, so you will need to try different things depending on your kitten's mood. Soft pâté or a spoon of baby food will tempt most cats, but use only foods that you know your kitten tolerates.

- Rewards must be timed to arrive just a moment after your kitten does the right behavior, so be alert and ready.
- Offer rewards regularly for small improvements, and don't expect too much too soon.

Clicker Training

Clicker training is a very popular training technique, which uses a small plastic gadget with a metal tongue that makes a clicking noise when it is depressed and released. The kitten is taught to associate the click sound with the arrival of a reward; this system is called operant conditioning. The click occurs when the kitten performs a desirable behavior. The click acts to

What I'd like my kitten to learn:	Rewards my kitten likes:

"mark" the action and lets the kitten know that she will now be rewarded. Begin by offering a reward and clicking as the kitten eats it. A loud click may startle your kitten, so either muffle the noise by holding the clicker up your sleeve or in your pocket, or try to purchase a quieter version.

Short training sessions will be enjoyable for both you and your kitten.

Possible goals for kitten training
- To come when she hears her name
- To tolerate grooming
- To scratch her own post
- To have her jump onto a table or chair
- To sit on command
- To wave her paws
- To fetch a toy

Example for training "Sit"
- Begin by holding the treat or toy near your kitten's nose.
- Slowly move the treat backward over your kitten's head so she raises her chin to follow the reward.
- Holding this position is difficult. A kitten's rear will eventually go down.
- As soon as she is in position, say "Sit."

You may have to reward this in stages during which the rear is lowered slightly before you achieve a real sit. Remember to say "Sit" only at the *moment* the desired behavior occurs.

Example for training "Wave"
- Begin by teaching a Sit command.
- Lure your kitten into position. Hold a treat a bit above her head.
- Wait for your kitten to raise her paws to reach for the reward.
- When she does, reward and say "Wave."
- Develop into a full wave without using a treat.

A SAFE AND STIMULATING ENVIRONMENT

From about 6 months of age, you may want to allow your kitten supervised outdoor access. Before you do, ensure that your kitten has had all necessary vaccinations and the area is as secure as possible. Take every precaution to keep your kitten safe.

Outdoor Safety

Securing Fencing—Encourage your kitten to remain in your yard by securing the borders to neighboring properties. It is possible to make fences harder to cross by adding wires or mesh at an angle into your own yard.

Cat Run—If you have a backyard, you may want to build an enclosed cat run. This is a safe enclosure where your cat can safely explore, sunbathe, climb, scratch, and watch the world go by.

Collar—Use one designed to break apart if tugged hard. This will protect your kitten if the collar should snag on something. A reflective collar will also make your kitten more visible to drivers. Add an ID tag with your cat's name and your name, phone, and address. This way you can be quickly contacted if your cat should escape or become lost.

Microchip ID—Keep microchip details up to date.

My kitten's microchip number is:

Microchip registry telephone number:

Protection from Other Cats—
Fights over neighborhood territory issues can lead to injury, distress and disease. Neutered males are less likely to get into fights. That said it is far too dangerous these days to allow cats access to the outdoors without supervision. Many dangers lurk outside, including feral cats with diseases, coyotes, roaming dogs, and speeding vehicles. Your cat is far safer being kept indoors and allowed outdoors when kept on a leash and harness or allowed to play inside an outdoor enclosure.

Outdoor Safety Ideas

- Always check greenhouses before you close them up. Ask neighbors to do the same, as a cat will quickly die from the extreme heat if trapped.
- Tidy up sheds so that your kitten does not come in to contact with toxic substances such as wood treatments (e.g., creosote), or petroleum-derived products. Both can cause irritation and burning to the skin and mouth. Keep weedkillers out of reach and sharp tools locked away.
- Garages pose many dangers. Antifreeze products are attractive to cats but are also highly poisonous to them. Make sure lids are securely fastened and spillages are cleaned up immediately.
- Check underneath your car before moving off. Cats will seek shelter and warmth beneath vehicles, especially on cooler days.
- If you own an inquisitive breed who likes to try to escape, tell your neighbors so they know whom to call if they discover your cat in their homes or car or spot her wandering in the street.
- Ponds can be dangerous to kittens. Cats are often attracted to them to drink or by the movement of fish. A kitten can easily drown in a pond, so make sure that yours is secured by taut netting or mesh. Loose pond coverings may be more dangerous than none at all since the kitten

If Your Kitten Gets Lost

Local animal control phone number:	
Local animal shelter phone number:	
When you last saw your kitten:	
Where you last saw your kitten:	
Identifying marks on your kitten:	

Harmful Plants Checklist

Plant	Poisonous Part	I own
Allium	Bulb	
Amaryllis	Bulb	
Azalea	Entire plant	
Bird of paradise	Seeds, fruit	
Castor oil plant	Entire plant	
Clematis	Entire plant	
Cyclamen	Flowers	
Foxglove	Entire plant	
Impatiens	Entire plant	
Iris	Tubers	
Ivy	Whole plants	
Laburnum	Flowers and seeds	
Larkspur	Entire plant	
Lily of the Valley	Entire plant	
Narcissus	Bulbs, stem	
Peace lily	Entire plant	
Rhododendron	Entire plant	
Snowdrop/Star of Bethlehem	Entire plant	
Wisteria	Seeds, pods	
Yew	Needles, seeds, bark	

Safety Tip

Keep a recent, clear photograph of your kitten so you can make posters to put up around your area and post on telephone poles.

could get tangled, preventing her from reaching the side again. Make sure that ponds have ledges or gradual slopes so any animal falling in can escape to safety.

Common Toxic Plants

It is not normally necessary to remove plants from your yard. However, some plants are highly toxic in small amounts, and these should be avoided. Some cats are more likely to chew on plants than others are. If your cat likes to explore and you are concerned, consider making a safe enclosure for your kitten since you cannot guarantee what your neighbors will grow. Identify the type of plants in your yard with an ID tag in the pots.

35

Indoor Environment

One feature that is paramount to a cat's happiness and health is a suitable living environment. Think of your home's interior from your kitten's perspective. This is easier if you have an understanding about normal feline behavior and habits.

An enriched environment has been shown to reduce the amount of behavioral problems that may arise, including aggression between cats. Creating a kitten paradise takes imagination and creativity, but will provide huge enjoyment and stimulation for your kitten, making it amply worth your time and effort.

Indoor Ideas Involving Food

It will be much more interesting for your kitten if she has to hunt around the house looking for surprise snacks rather than just getting a bowl of food in the same place every day. Place food and water bowls in different areas, especially if you have more than one cat. Your kitten will enjoy foraging for food from randomly positioned activity toys stuffed with tempting morsels. Split your kitten's daily food into several small batches throughout the day.

left: **Cats seek out raised areas on which to rest and contentedly watch the world go by.**

Example of Activity Toy	Suggested Use
Cardboard box	Mix a layer of scrunched paper with some treats to encourage your cat to forage around inside the box. Catnip toys can also be hidden away inside.
Plastic bottle	Cut several holes into the bottle and fill it with dry food. You can either leave on the floor for your kitten to bat about or hang it up to encourage stretching.
Empty ice-cream carton	Rinse and dry thoroughly first. Then cut large holes into the sides or top to encourage your kitten to reach inside to scoop out the treats.
Toilet paper roll stuffed with scrunched paper	Include tasty treats inside the scrunched paper to tempt your kitten to bat and pounce and tear it open. These can be hung up to encourage stretching.
Kong food toy	A hard, hollow rubber toy that can be filled with morsels of food to encourage interest.

above:
Simple
paper toys can
provide lots of
fantastic fun.

above: **Cats love looking out of windows.**
However, nervous cats may be stressed by
seeing roaming cats and begin spray marking.

left: Ensure that all small, vulnerable pets
are kept safely away from your kitten.

Indoor Ideas Involving Spaces

People normally assess a room by the amount of
floor space available to move about in. A kitten
views the same room in terms of both floor space
and the vertical spaces where they can climb.
Raised positions are attractive, as cats can watch
the world go by while feeling safe. These areas are
very important in a multicat household but are
equally necessary for a single cat in order to
introduce variety and provide resting places.

Creating more places for your cat to hide in,
sit on, climb up, and jump off is important, but
there are other ways to entertain your kitten.

Social contact is important, so make sure that
your kitten gets enough play and petting time
with you every day. Another kitten will help to
keep him occupied, but your attention is
important.

Visual Stimulation—Videos can keep a kitten
amused. There are DVDs with footage of birds
and fish that you can play for your kitten's
amusement. An aquarium will also provide your
kitten with some movement to observe, although
you must make sure that the lid is strong and any
lighting or heating cables are secure. Blocking off
access to the lid is the safest option if your kitten
will be unsupervised around a fish tank.

Scent Trails—Felines have a keen sense of smell.
Buy catnip toys or make one by stuffing an old
sock with rags and some catnip herb. Then create
a scent trail by rubbing the toy or a treat along a
route in the house and then leaving the toy or
tidbit for your kitten to find. Make this easy at first,
but once your kitten gets the hang of it, make it
more challenging.

Enriching the Outdoor Environment

Although the world outdoors provides your kitten with lots of interesting sights, sounds, and smells, it must be safe. Depending on where you live, there are different options to make sure that cats have a chance to enjoy their outdoor spaces.

Gardens—Although cats are known carnivores (meat eaters), some enjoy munching on greens. Consider reserving some space in your backyard garden to grow cat-friendly plants such as rye grass, catnip, and catmint. Make sure not to use any harmful pesticides or herbicides in your yard to protect the health of your kitten.

Enclosures—A sure way to give your cat safe outdoor access is by providing an enclosure. Cats will enjoy having their own enclosure, whether it be built over a balcony, against your home, or as a separate building altogether. Whatever space you have will add another dimension to the lives of those who would otherwise live indoors only.

Enclosures can be bought in kit form or even homemade. There are many examples of fantastic cat runs and enclosures to fit all spaces on the Internet. Remember to only use cat-friendly products for your run. You also want them to be secure enough to protect your cat against predators such as coyotes and roaming dogs.

Within this safe space, your kitten should be able to perform many natural feline behaviors that will help him feel more contented. He will be able to watch birds and insects, scratch on the posts, relax in the sunshine, and exercise by climbing.

Items to include in an enclosure:

- Large cat tree or sturdy, elevated platform to perch and catnap
- Upright logs to climb on and scratch
- Fresh water and possibly food
- A bathroom area (perhaps sand, soil, or bark chips depending on your cat's preference) or litter box
- Access back into your home in case of inclement weather

left: **Your cat will appreciate a pot of catmint, which he can smell, touch, and chew.**

below: **Kittens are born explorers, so take care if they are likely to play around watering cans.**

- Greenery to provide cover and shade
- Toy mice or other favorite playthings

Harness and lead—If you have an active cat who loves the outdoors but an enclosure isn't possible, perhaps because you live in an apartment or condo, then you may want to try training your kitten to walk on a harness and lead. Using these will enable you to accompany your kitten while allowing him to explore the outdoors a few times a week. Ensure that your kitten is familiar with the harness before you attempt to take him outside. It is essential that the harness fits well to prevent your kitten from wriggling out and escaping. Always reinforce your kitten's acceptance of these items with praise.

below: **A secure outdoor garden will provide an exciting extension to your kitten's home environment.**

above: **Outdoor areas provide options for scratching and climbing as the kitten exercises.**

MY KITTEN'S DIET

Whether you obtain your kitten from a breeder, from an animal shelter, from a breed rescue group, or as a stray from the streets, it is important that you work with your vet to select a high-quality commercial food best suited to meet your kitten's specific needs. Some breeders will provide food samples in their kitten pack. Avoid making any abrupt changes in diet.

Take your kitten to your vet for a complete examination within a few days of his arrival. Your vet will be able to give you advice about suitable diets and about the correct amounts to feed your kitten. It is useful for your kitten to be gradually introduced to different flavors and textures of food so that he does not become a finicky eater as an adult.

A Diet Plan for the First Year

Kittens need to take in lots of fuel to allow them to grow and exercise. However, their stomachs are very small, so they need several small meals each day. If you can't be around to personally provide all of the meals, you could try using a time-release bowl or at least leave some dry food in a bowl for the kitten to graze on while you are away.

As your kitten grows, the amount of food he requires and the frequency of his meals will change. The specifics of how much to feed and how often will depend upon how well your kitten is growing and how energetic he is. You can complete the table on the next page according to the instructions you receive from your vet and from the guidelines included with your kitten's food. Observe your kitten and try to maintain a healthy body shape by increasing or decreasing his food intake according to his body condition (see pages 42–43). Between 6 and 12 months of age, your kitten will be able to eat larger meals and won't require as many meals during the day. Over the course of a few days, drop down to

Veterinarian's Recommended Diet on Collection

You can attach your veterinarian's diet plan here or fill in the recommendations for each of your kitten's meals during the day. All kittens should have fresh water to drink at all times. It helps to place more than one bowl around the home to encourage your kitten to drink.

First Meal	Second Meal	Third Meal	Fourth Meal	Fifth Meal
Time:	Time:	Time:	Time:	Time:

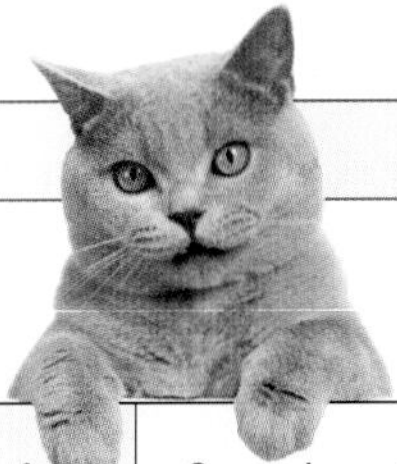

Diet Record

	First meal consists of:	Second meal consists of:	Third meal consists of:
3–5 months			
6–12 months			

feeding two meals by slightly increasing the amount offered in those meals and reducing the amount in the one you wish to skip. Then adjust the remaining meals to the appropriate amounts.

Wean your kitten onto an adult food when he reaches one year of age. At this point, he will be physically fully grown. Prior to this age, he needs the nutrition and energy contained in a specific kitten diet.

Assessing Your Kitten's Diet

Once your kitten has settled in and is successfully using the litter box, you may want to change the type of food you provide. If you are changing your kitten's diet, make sure to choose a high-quality commercial food that provides your kitten with all the nutrients he will require for his growth and development. Read the label to check that the product contains animal-derived proteins, low levels of carbohydrates and fat, the necessary vitamins, and the appropriate amino acids.

Switching to a New Food

Change your kitten's diet over a period of 7 to 10 days. Replace increasingly larger portions of the old diet with the new food until the swap has been made entirely. Mix the two foods thoroughly before offering it to your kitten. You can take longer to swap the foods if you want or if your kitten has a sensitive tummy. If your kitten has loose stools on the new food, then either you have made the change too quickly, or he is not able to tolerate this particular food.

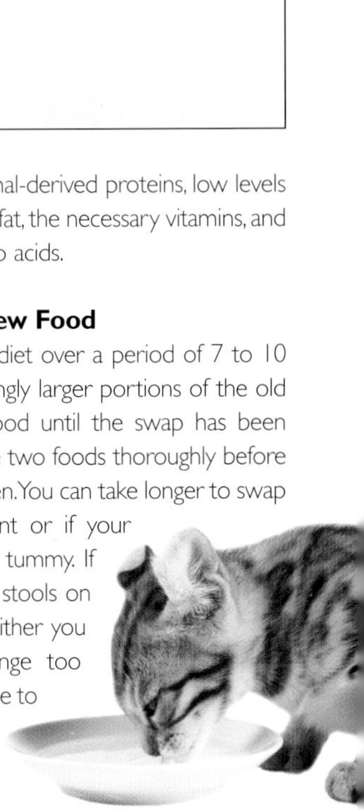

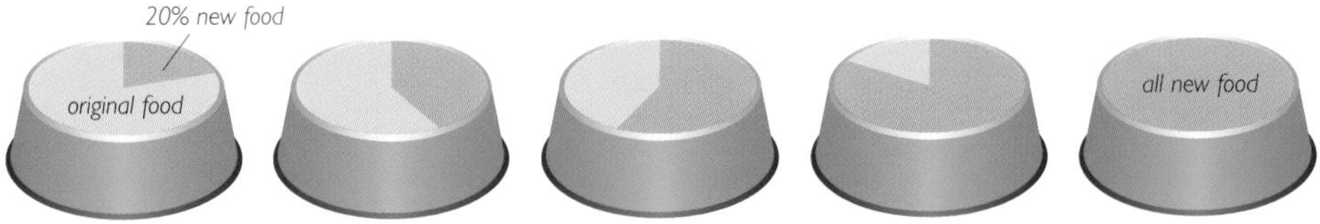

Day 1–2	Day 3–4	Day 5–6	Day 7–8	Day 9
80% original food 20% new food	60% original food 40% new food	40% original food 60% new food	20% original food 80% new food	On 100% new food

Maintaining Your Kitten's Weight

Obesity is becoming one of the major health issues affecting pet cats. Although cats normally monitor their intake of food to balance their energy requirement, some will overeat. Overeating is more common in cats who are bored and inactive.

Many owners overfeed their pets because they misunderstand what pets need. A meowing cat is often interpreted as being hungry when he may simply be signaling a greeting, or a desire to play or to be petted. Owners are often trained to respond to a cat's demands, too. A bored cat will quickly learn that by meowing loudly, his owner will eventually offer him food. Some cat foods are highly appetizing but also highly fattening.

How Much to Feed

Although the diet you buy will have a feeding guide printed on the side, you will have to monitor this yourself to some extent. This is because all cats vary in their growth and energy expenditure. It may be appropriate to reduce the amount you feed slightly. If your cat suddenly gains or loses weight without an obvious reason, ask your vet to examine him.

Your kitten's weight will depend upon his breed and sex. Your vet and breeder will be able to tell you about the correct weight range for your kitten. Regularly check your kitten's weight, and try to stay within the appropriate range.

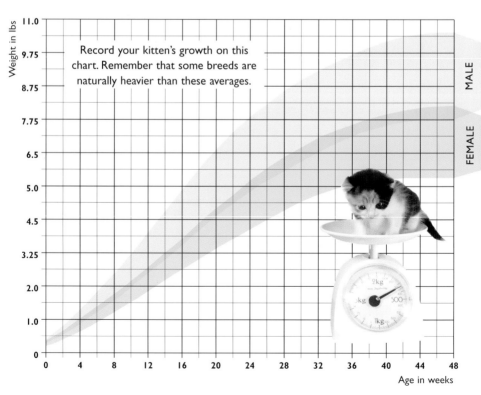

Record your kitten's growth on this chart. Remember that some breeds are naturally heavier than these averages.

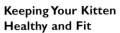

Keeping Your Kitten Healthy and Fit

- Monitor growth and weight gain, and alter the amount fed appropriately.
- Encourage your kitten to play energetically with you at least twice a day.
- Encourage your kitten to be active, either in a safe, supervised area outside or within his enclosure every day.
- Stop the family from feeding excess treats.
- Use any treats for training only and reduce the main meals a little to compensate for these extra treats.
- Stop houseguests from offering extra food.

below: **The five body condition scores describe a cat's physical condition with 3 being ideal. If your cat scores differently, consider why he is carrying too much or too little weight.**

Body Condition Score

Body condition scores are used by vets and other professionals to monitor the physical condition of a cat. Your cat's body shape is a great indicator of whether he is under- or overweight. Since owners may find it difficult to weigh their cat regularly, body condition can be used as a simple indicator for cats of all ages. A change in your cat's body condition may alert you to a medical problem or signal that you are feeding too much or too little.

Complete this table as your kitten grows to allow you to monitor how much you've been feeding and how rapidly your kitten has gained weight and to ensure he is in optimal body condition along the way. This will help you recognize the early signs of any problems as well as allow you to look back and consider why your cat is not in ideal shape—should that eventually occur.

1	2	3	4	5

 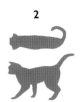   

Kitten's Age	Weight	Body Condition Score	Amount of Food per Day (following diet guidelines)
3 months			
6 months			
9 months			
12 months			

1 *Emaciated—ribs visible on short haired cats, no palpable fat*

2 *Thin—ribs easily palpable with minimal fat covering*

3 *Ideal—observable waist, well-proportioned*

4 *Heavy—waist not discernible, obvious rounding of abdomen*

5 *Obese—heavy fat deposits, distended abdomen, no waist*

HEALTH CARE

Your kitten should be taken to your vet for a physical exam and necessary vaccinations within a few days of being adopted. It is important that your vet examine your kitten thoroughly to assure you that he is healthy. It is also a great socialization experience for your kitten.

Your vet will then advise you of when to return for your kitten's vaccination appointments, how often and with what products you should worm and flea-treat your kitten, and about diets and growth. It is valuable experience for your kitten to attend the clinic even when no treatments are necessary so he can get used to the unfamiliar smells, sights, and sounds.

Getting Used to Veterinary Experiences

It can be difficult to prepare your kitten for a visit to the vet, but there are things that you can do to be prepared and to reduce the likelihood of a stressful visit. A kitten who is socialized thoroughly will be happier overall, so make sure that you focus lots of time on this during the early months. The following experiences can also be practiced at home:

Traveling in cat carrier—Kittens who only leave the home when they require veterinary treatment are more likely to feel anxious and resist handling when they arrive at the vet clinic. Get your kitten used to getting into his carrier and riding in the car. This is especially important if you plan to travel with your kitten later on.

Being examined on the table—Make sure that some of your grooming and petting occurs on a table so that your kitten is not shocked when placed on one by the vet. Kittens need to be safely introduced to elevated platforms. Use treats to reinforce a positive experience.

Record of Ailments

Date:	Date:
Problem:	Problem:
Treatment:	Treatment:
Points to note for future reference:	Points to note for future reference:

Date:	Date:
Problem:	Problem:
Treatment:	Treatment:
Points to note for future reference:	Points to note for future reference:

Record of Vaccinations

Date	Vaccination Given	

Having ears and mouth examined—Your kitten will grow up allowing you to check his ears and mouth if done slowly and carefully with plenty of rewards for good behavior. First, make sure your kitten is happy to be handled and petted by you. Stand behind your kitten with one hand on his chest to stop him from moving away. Gently move the kitten's head to give you the best view, and very gently pull the ear backward until you can see inside. Praise your kitten immediately and reward him for allowing you to do this. Then check the second ear. Do this regularly until your kitten is totally comfortable.

The mouth can be trickier, but it gets easier with practice. Gently tip your kitten's head back a little while you pet him. Using your thumb and forefinger, gently lift your kitten's lips to reveal the teeth. It can help to run your finger over the teeth to the back so you can see them all. A kitten finger brush and cat toothpaste can help some kittens overcome any resistance to mouth exams. Over time, you can begin to gently open the mouth, too. Do this very briefly before praising and offering your kitten his favorite treat.

Having an allover body examination—A kitten who is used to being petted will usually allow you to run your hands all over his body. Get him used to you gently feeling his abdomen and checking under his tail. A kitten you hope to show will have to be confident during handling to show himself at his best.

Tell your vet about any concerns.

Vet checks are important to maintain good kitten care.

Dealing with Parasites

All animals can be infected with parasites. Kittens can carry both internal parasites and external parasites contracted from the mother's milk, their environment, or their food. Various species of parasitic worm can live in the bowel and intestines, while mites, fleas, and ticks live on the outside of the body.

Parasites can make your kitten seriously ill and can spread dangerous diseases to other pets as well as to humans. Larvae can remain dormant in the cat's body throughout his life, so it is important to treat your kitten and any adult cats for parasites on a regular basis.

Worming

The breeder or animal rescue should have wormed your kitten before you bring him home. Ask for the details (see pages 10–11) so you can accurately inform your vet. Your vet will then advise you about which wormer to use in the future and how often. There are products

above: **Regular flea prevention will ensure that your kitten doesn't spread these parasites.**

available without prescription from supermarkets and pet stores, but these are often less effective. You also must be careful to avoid any product

My Kitten's Worming Chart

Date of worming:	Date of worming:
Product used:	Product used:
Any side effects noted:	Any side effects noted:
Date of worming:	Date of worming:
Product used:	Product used:
Any side effects noted:	Any side effects noted:
Date of worming:	Date of worming:
Product used:	Product used:
Any side effects noted:	Any side effects noted:
right: A *Taenia* tapeworm that infests cats can grow up to 2 feet long. 	Date of worming:
	Product used:
	Any side effects noted:

My Kitten's Flea Prevention Chart

Date of treatment: Product used: Any side effects noted:	Date of treatment: Product used: Any side effects noted:
Date of treatment: Product used: Any side effects noted:	Date of treatment: Product used: Any side effects noted:
Date of treatment: Product used: Any side effects noted:	Date of treatment: Product used: Any side effects noted:
Date of treatment: Product used: Any side effects noted:	Date of treatment: Product used: Any side effects noted:

Flea Problems Within the Home

Fleas were noticed in:
I was bitten by fleas in:
Product used to treat household soft furnishings and carpets:
Treatment date:
Repeat treatment date:

containing Permethrin, as it is toxic to cats (although used commonly in dog wormers). How often you worm your kitten will depend upon his lifestyle. Does your cat have outdoor access? Live with other cats? Consult your vet for the best treatment plan. Also seek advice if you are traveling to an area where **whipworm**, **hookworm**, or **heartworm** may be present, as your kitten will require different products.

Tick Removal

If you spot a tick feeding on your cat, try to remove it before it can drop off and multiply. You can purchase a special tick remover from your vet or pet store. These allow you to remove the tick without breaking or crushing it, which could increase the chances of infection. Afterward, wipe the area with pet-friendly disinfectant, and wash your hands thoroughly.

Recognizing Signs of Illness or Injury

Cats are able to cover up minor illness or injuries surprisingly well. This ability serves to protect them from being singled out as weak or vulnerable by predators or competitors. Unfortunately, it also means that early signs of illness may be missed by a nonvigilant owner.

There will be varied signs of illness or injury, depending on what is wrong with your kitten. Getting to know what is normal for your pet is important.

- Regular handling familiarizes you with his normal body condition.
- Playing tells you about his normal energy and activity levels.
- Monitoring food and water intake informs you about his normal appetite.
- Monitoring stool formation and amount of urine in litter box familiarizes you with your kitten's normal motions.
- Tracking your kitten's weight allows you to know what is normal for your kitten and makes early changes easier to detect.

Any changes in the above features could indicate a health problem. Your kitten may seem a little lethargic or quieter than normal, or he may have less appetite. If the change is mild and not affecting your kitten's overall behavior, then observe it carefully over a few hours to a day. If there is no improvement, then seek veterinary advice. Be concerned if you notice a pronounced increase in your cat hiding or having bathroom accidents. Any severe changes or signs of blood in urine or feces should be brought to your vet's attention immediately. As the owner of your kitten, you will know his normal behavior better than anyone. If you're feeling concerned, then seek help, since an illness that is detected early is almost always easier to treat; and if you're given the "all clear," then you've saved yourself a lot of needless worry and sleepless nights.

Preparing for Potential Problems

While illness and accidents are a part of life, it is best to be prepared. Taking good care of your kitten through appropriate treatments, a healthy diet, and a stimulating environment is the best way to avoid many problems. However, there are some unavoidable conditions that may crop up in some cats and that will require treatment.

above: **Changes in your cat's drinking or eating habits will alert you to early signs of illness.**

above: **Inflamed third eyelids or runny eyes should be checked by your vet without delay.**

Inherited Conditions

When you were researching your chosen breed, you might have discovered certain problems that are prevalent within that type of cat. Choosing your kitten carefully from a responsible breeder who breeds only cats who have been tested for these conditions and have passed their health checks is important. This will make it less likely that your kitten will carry a problematic gene. However, not all diseases are easy to track, so you should research thoroughly and discuss any concerns with the major feline organizations and a feline veterinary specialist to make sure you are fully aware of what to look out for.

Commonly inherited diseases in my kitten's breed:

Action I took to reduce the likelihood of the problem in my kitten:

Insurance for Your Kitten

Veterinary care can be costly, especially over the lifetime of your cat if he develops an ongoing condition. It is possible to purchase insurance to protect you from the unexpected cost from an accident or illness. Policies vary, so it is important to research carefully. Cheaper policies may initially seem attractive but may cover far fewer conditions, have a limit to their payout amount, or may offer coverage only until your cat reaches a certain age. Some pedigree breeds will not be covered for commonly inherited conditions. It pays to make sure you choose a comprehensive policy that suits your situation.

Chosen insurance company:

Policy number:

Claims line telephone number:

left: Vaccinations are a vital part of disease prevention.

below: A quiet kitten may be feeling unwell.

49

Dealing with Injury or Illness

Cause for Concern	Remedy/Action to Take
Road traffic accident	**Seek urgent veterinary help.** • Make sure your kitten's airways are open. • Carefully place your kitten on a blanket or coat to support him while you travel to the vet. If you have your cat carrier or a box to transport the kitten in, this will help to minimize movement and prevent further injury. • Keeping the kitten in a quiet and darkened place will help reduce further distress while you travel.
Appetite change	• If you have changed the diet or the product's recipe has changed, then observe your kitten. It may be necessary to revert to the original food and make any change-over more slowly. • Sudden changes, especially when accompanied by the opposite weight loss/gain than would be expected, should be brought to your vet's attention. • Gently examine your kitten's mouth to make sure there's nothing stuck between the teeth that could be easily removed. • If your kitten is tolerant of being handled, check for broken or cracked teeth. • Your vet should examine your kitten if you have any concerns.
Lameness/difficulty moving/inability to jump up	• Gently examine limbs for swelling, cuts, or thorns. Prickly plants caught in the coat can be removed. Any injury, swelling, or hot joints should be checked by your vet. • Overweight cats should be placed on a diet to reduce strain on the joints. Your veterinarian will be able to provide advice about pet weight loss.
Coat change	Any loss of condition should be brought to your vet's attention since this can signal an array of problems that are best dealt with early on. If your kitten is grooming or scratching excessively, then you should check that his parasite control treatments are up to date. If the problem continues, seek veterinary advice.
Cat fight	When your kitten has calmed down after the fight, gently examine him from head to toe. If your kitten is bleeding, you should carefully bathe the wounds in a warm saline solution. Bite wounds should be given careful attention. Although they're often small, they often develop into abscesses from the bacteria present in a cat's mouth. Seek veterinary help if the bite is deep, is weeping discharge, or appears swollen and red. Antibiotics will probably be required.

Cause for Concern	Remedy/Action to Take
Poisoning	Seek urgent veterinary help. If possible, tell the staff what your kitten has consumed when you call them so they can find out about the product and be prepared. Take any product packaging with you if you know what toxin your kitten has ingested. ● Do not try to make your kitten vomit. ● Try to prevent your kitten from licking any more substance from his feet or coat during your trip to the clinic by wrapping him in a blanket.
Problems with eyes	Weeping or swollen eyes should be examined as soon as possible. Causes vary from a simple irritation to a foreign body, an abscess, or even cat flu. ● Carefully bathing your kitten's eye in warm water may allow you to identify the problem, but veterinary advice is essential.
Vomiting 	**Fur balls**: Cats who ingest too much hair while grooming themselves may vomit up the excess in the form of matted fur balls. ● Increase the time you spend grooming your kitten to allow maximum removal of excess hair. **Foodstuffs**: There are many causes for vomiting. ● If severe or accompanied by diarrhea or lethargy, then visit vet urgently. ● Observe your kitten and note down any other changes that may be relevant. ● Note down how long after eating or drinking your kitten is sick and how often this occurs. ● Occasional cases with no other concerning signs can often be remedied by providing a light diet and close observation to check for further symptoms.
Seizure	Seizures can be caused by several different triggers, including poisons, head trauma, or disease. If you think your cat has ingested a toxic substance, your vet will need to know what this is, so take the product and packaging with you. If your cat is seizing, you should: ● Secure the area by closing doors and windows. ● Place your kitten on a soft blanket and move items that your kitten may injure himself on. ● Make the situation as quiet as possible by turning off televisions or music and staying calm. Close the curtains and dim the lights if possible. ● Call your veterinarian and explain what you have seen, for how long it has been going on, and any potential causes.

NEUTERING AND SPAYING ADVICE

Kitten growth and development is continuous throughout the early months. Physically, you'll notice your kitten's adult teeth coming through and his size and shape gradually changing into the adult form. Although different breeds develop at slightly different rates, most reach their physical size between 12 and 18 months.

Between the ages of approximately 6 and 12 months, your kitten will reach sexual maturity, so it is important to closely monitor any intact kittens. Female sexual maturity has been found to be linked to a combination of factors, including the presence of tomcats, the season, and whether other females are in season.

Changes in Behavior

As your kitten reaches adulthood, his behavior will change. If he has not been neutered, then you can expect more pronounced behavioral changes such as increased territorial aggression. Physical looks also change; intact tomcats grow thicker hair around the neck and develop a stockier shape.

Mature Males

Territory—This becomes more important, and your cat may patrol more and react aggressively toward intruding cats. This is the age when you may begin to notice him spray marking around the yard or within the home.

Courtship—A male will be attracted to females in heat around your home. Your cat may begin to caterwaul around the female cat's location. Males in search of females will roam far and wide and will be more likely to try to chase off any competing suitors.

Mating—Your male kitten will be able to mate successfully at a surprisingly young age. There are breed differences, with some Oriental types successfully mating at just a few months of age.

right: **Mature males may pick fights with intruders.**

Health Benefits of Neutering Your Kitten

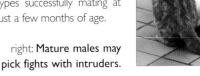

Disease Transmission	Neutered cats fight less and so are less likely to contract FeLV and FIV among other diseases.
Avoidable Illness	Spayed females are less likely to develop mammary cancers than are those who have had seasons.
	Spayed females avoid ovarian and uterine cancers.
	Spayed females avoid a potentially fatal condition called pyometra, which is caused by a bacterial infection within the uterus.
	Neutered males avoid testicular cancer.
Reduced Injury	Neutered cats are less likely to fight and suffer from resulting bite abscesses and scratches.

Questions to Consider

Do I want to breed my kitten?	☐ Yes ☐ No
Do I want to show my kitten?	☐ Yes ☐ No
Do I have a breeding agreement with my kitten's breeder?	☐ Yes ☐ No

*If you answer **Yes** to any of the above you **shouldn't** neuter/spay your kitten.*

Do I have entire cats of the opposite sex to consider?	☐ Yes ☐ No
Is there any chance my kitten will meet another cat and mate?	☐ Yes ☐ No
Does my kitten's contract include a neutering/spaying agreement?	☐ Yes ☐ No
Was my kitten sold as being unsuitable to breed from?	☐ Yes ☐ No

*If you answer **Yes** to any of the above you **should** neuter/spay your kitten.*

Is my kitten of good enough quality to breed from?	☐ Yes ☐ No
Do I have money and time to ensure that all medical checks are done before mating my cat?	☐ Yes ☐ No
Do I have time and money to care for a litter?	☐ Yes ☐ No
Can I find suitable homes for all the kittens?	☐ Yes ☐ No

*If you answer **No** to any of the above you **should** neuter/spay your kitten.*

Having considered the above questions, I have decided ☐ Yes ☐ No to neuter/spay my kitten.

Mature Females

Territory—This is also more important to adult females than juveniles, and the territorial instinct is more intense in those with kittens.

Vocalization—This typically increases while the female is in season, and the calling may last continuously for many minutes. This is to attract male suitors but can annoy neighbors.

Urine marking—Such behavior is common in females in season. This acts to signal her presence and to attract potential mates.

Maternal aggression—This may occur if the female feels threatened while nursing kittens but should subside as the kittens age. Improve the situation by providing a low-stress environment and keeping visitors to a minimum.

TRAVEL TIPS

Most cat owners have to find alternative care for their cats while they are away from home, whether that be just for a few days or several weeks.

While there are several care options available (see *The Owner's Handbook* pages 58–59), many owners choose to use a pet sitter or boarding facility. Finding the right one will ease any worries you may have while you're away.

Checklist of Points to Consider When Choosing a Boarding Facility

Staff are friendly and knowledgeable	❏ Yes	❏ No
There are sufficient members of staff to care for the animals	❏ Yes	❏ No
I can look around the place in advance	❏ Yes	❏ No
The facilities are clean and fresh	❏ Yes	❏ No
The cats have spacious pens with access to a secure run	❏ Yes	❏ No
The cats have plenty of opportunity for privacy within their runs	❏ Yes	❏ No
The staff follow a strict health and safety policy	❏ Yes	❏ No
My cat has up-to-date vaccinations	❏ Yes	❏ No
I believe my kitten will feel happy in this cattery	❏ Yes	❏ No
Additional Points		
I'm willing to travel.....................miles to the right place.		
My budget for boarding is.....................per night.		

Some owners feel happier leaving their kittens at home in the care of another person while they are away. While some people are lucky enough to have a family member living close by; others will need to rely on a professional pet sitter to tend to their kittens while they are away. Taking time to get some reliable recommendations and to make sure the person is suited to you and your kitten is important.

Checklist of Points to Consider When Choosing a Professional Pet Sitter

The sitter is friendly and knowledgeable	☐ Yes	☐ No
The sitter has adequate time to focus on my kitten's care	☐ Yes	☐ No
The sitter will visit in advance and spend time discussing my requirements	☐ Yes	☐ No
The sitter has taken detailed notes about what will be required	☐ Yes	☐ No
The sitter behaves in an appropriate manner with my kitten	☐ Yes	☐ No
The sitter can provide satisfactory references	☐ Yes	☐ No
The sitter has been police-checked	☐ Yes	☐ No
The sitter is licensed and insured	☐ Yes	☐ No
The sitter knows about any health problems my kitten has and is happy to administer treatment and/or look for signs of recurrence	☐ Yes	☐ No
I believe my kitten will feel happy with this person	☐ Yes	☐ No
Additional Points		
My budget for a pet sitter is..................per day / night		

TEACHING GOOD BEHAVIOR

Using the Cat Door

Once your kitten is old enough, you may wish him to use a cat door to go out to a safe enclosure. Some owners manage to fit a cat door into a secured outer run or window enclosure.

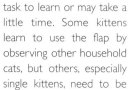

Depending on your kitten, this can be an easy task to learn or may take a little time. Some kittens learn to use the flap by observing other household cats, but others, especially single kittens, need to be taught how the flap works. There is often a little nervousness around the flap to begin with, but as long as it is introduced in a pleasant way, this initial reluctance should quickly diminish. Be patient when teaching your kitten how to work the flap.

Introducing the flap is simplest if you have one that swings open easily when the kitten pushes it. This means that any attempt your kitten makes is more likely to be successful. If he tries and fails to open the flap, he might not continue to attempt to push through. When your kitten is very small, he may find it easier to push through by pressing against the bottom of the flap, where less force is required. If you are showing or luring your kitten to push, try to aim for low down, perhaps at a corner. Some kittens can be lured to try this if you sit at the other side and call them. Make sure that you are ready with a tasty treat as a reward.

Other kittens need a more gradual introduction to the cat flap. You can string the flap open so your kitten learns about passing through the open gap. Gradually lower the flap by a few inches over several sessions so your kitten gets used to pushing through bit by bit. Place some enticing treats on the other side so your kitten is rewarded for his efforts. You can also encourage your kitten to push back through into the house by using one of his meals inside as the reward.

Be patient and never force your kitten through the cat flap. If he is nervous, perhaps there is a good reason for his anxiety. Something on the outside could be worrying your kitten; this can be the presence of other cats, their spray marks, loud noises, or just the overall unfamiliarity. Make sure you have introduced your kitten to the outside area first by accompanying him for short sessions and working on his socialization.

Preventing and Coping with Demanding Behavior

A kitten can quickly learn ways to get you to respond to him. Many kittens will use vocalization to make their owners respond since this tends to work well. However, many owners then become upset because of their kitten's excessive noise. Of course, the easiest way to prevent this problem is to be careful how you respond to and interact with your kitten from the start.

While some kittens will learn just to meow prior to mealtimes, others will begin to call when they also wish for interaction with their owner. In some of the more vocal breeds, this can quickly become problematic, although all cats can learn to be overdemanding. Noisy demands are particularly troublesome if they occur, as many do, in the middle of the night. Since cats don't have the same sleeping and waking cycles as humans do, there is often a period in the night when the kitten is awake and wanting a game or some petting. Ignoring your kitten's demands is critical if you want to extinguish the behavior. However, this does not mean that your kitten should not be given adequate amounts of suitable interaction. It is critical that he is kept busy since many behavioral problems actually stem from the cat being understimulated, and bored. As with any behavior or training, praise and respond to your kitten when he is behaving in a way you like.

If your kitten is overdemanding, make sure that he has plenty of appropriate stimulation and lots of chances to interact with you every day. Leave interesting toys and small meals for your kitten to discover on his own, instead of having to rely on you throughout the day.

Be prepared for your kitten to initially try harder to get your attention. This is because he has learned that meowing works well, and it takes time for habits to change. Be consistent and respond to behaviors you like, and your kitten will soon make the change. Make sure everyone in the family is following the same rules, though, or this habit will take a very long time to break.

above: **Plan ahead and create an interesting environment for your kitten. It will help alleviate excessive demands for your attention.**

A catnip toy can be a very attractive lure.

Make sure that your kitten enjoys using the cat flap by offering his favorite treats and games as a reward for coming through.

Dealing with Urine Spraying

As your kitten matures, it is possible that he will begin urine spraying, particularly if you own an entire male. Females can also mark with urine, particularly when in season. Normally, spray marking is done around the outside periphery of the territory, but occasionally it will occur inside,

above: **Urine spray is pungent and difficult to clean, so indoor spraying problems require immediate attention.**

especially in cats who are kept indoors or with little access to the outside. Neutering makes a significant difference in the amount of spraying and will remove any hormonal cause for spraying. Around 90 percent to 95 percent of cats will stop spraying once neutered.

Other cats are probably responding to their environments. Spraying is often a sign of stress in the cat, which can have an array of causes. It is important to consider carefully any changes within the home in the months before the problem first manifested itself.

You will have to try to make changes to relax your cat again. Make sure he has enough safe places to which to retreat and lots of pleasant interactions. The use of a stress-lowering feline pheromone spray can also help reduce the incidence of spray marking. This is available from your vet clinic or pet supply store.

Cleaning up the spray marks properly is very important. If they remain, the next time your cat comes by, he is likely to mark the spot again, or another cat may be encouraged to begin marking. Feline urine marks are designed to last, and they have a greasy component that makes them more durable. There are many commercial cleaning products available. Seek ones that contain protein enzymatic cleaners, as they are designed to remove the stain and the scent. Always test any product first to ensure that no damage is done to your furniture or home. Spray marking can become a huge problem, so addressing the problem early is important. If you are unsure about the reasons for spraying or how to tackle it, ask your vet to refer you to a behaviorist.

Reducing Tension Between Cats

Not all cats will immediately accept a new kitten into their homes. The way that you introduce your new kitten is important and can either make the meetings amicable or create instant problems. Social experience is important, so if your original cat is aggressive toward all other cats, then it is unlikely to be a smooth introduction. Normally, it will take a week or two for things to settle down between the cats once you have introduced a new kitten, but occasionally, tensions can escalate. An indoor kennel can be useful for the initial introduction, as it will protect your kitten from the adult. Over time, the cats should

right: **Fighting between cats leads to increased tension and doesn't normally resolve itself.**

become used to seeing one another and will relax enough for you to open the door and allow them to meet.

Some aggression problems don't begin until the kitten approaches maturity, while others are related to the stress of a house move or changes in the family. If your cats have just suddenly started fighting, then you should ask your vet to examine them, as pain or illness can also cause irritability.

Be aware of the signals your cats are giving to each other. You will have to be very observant, as prior to full-blown fighting there will be tell-tale signs, such as staring and increased tension in the body. This is when it's most useful to stop the aggression by creating a distraction such as clapping your hands. Then place something between the cats. Don't allow the cats to fight it out, as this will not stop the aggression. Cats don't have a clear hierarchy system, and if they have no choice but to be around one another, they will probably avoid future aggression.

above: **Place separate food bowls well apart to ensure that each cat can relax while eating.**

Neutering the young cat will help to reduce any competitive aggression although it is still important to provide the cats with enough resources (such as bowls, litter boxess and sleeping areas) so they don't have to compete.

Scents and Sensibility

Group smell is important and is normally maintained by allo-grooming (where members of the same social group groom one another). If the cats aren't that closely bonded, then you can try to strengthen their relationship. Every day, rub each cat down with a very slightly damp cloth while you pet him, paying particular attention to the facial areas. This will allow you to transfer the scents onto one another, helping create a group scent as if the cats had spent time grooming each other. This will increase familiarity and may trigger genuine allo-grooming. Feline pheromone sprays available from your vet can also help calm the cats down.

It is often necessary to reintroduce the cats to one another slowly, although if the aggression is severe and if you can't be there to supervise while the cats are together, it may be kindest to consider rehoming one of the cats. A behaviorist can help you address this problem. If you ignore it, ongoing stress is likely to result in new problems, such as lack of interest in food, depression, overgrooming, eliminating in inappropriate places, and urine spraying.

INDEX

PICTURE CREDITS

Bayer HealthCare: 46 bottom left, 47 center right.

Jane Burton, Warren Photographic: Back cover top left, back cover bottom right, 3, 8 (all four images), 10 top right, 14 bottom, 19 bottom right, 23 top right, 27 top right, 29 center, 31 top, 32 left, 45 top right, 46 top, 48 bottom right, 57 bottom, 58 top left, 58-59.

Crestock.com:
Norman Chan: 2. Adrian Costea: 5 center right. Roxana Gonzalez: 55 bottom right. Iofoto studio: 21 (apple). Eric Isselée: 7, 10 left, 11 top right, 12, 13, 23 bottom right, 24 top right (kitten), 24 bottom right, 25 center left, 33 top center, 33 center (kitten), 33 bottom center, 34 bottom, 37 top left, 42 top center, 43, 44, 55 bottom center. Frenck Danielle Kaufmann: 18 top center. Rafa Irusta Machin: 4 top, 49 bottom right, 63. Monia Nilsen: 28 top right. Nikolai Okhitin: 6, 35 top, 39 top. Christopher Pounds: 40. Kristian Sekulic: Cover back flap, 22 bottom. Dusan Zidar: 4 bottom.

Dreamstime.com:
Stefan Andronache: 50 bottom left. Ivanov Arkady: 21 bottom right. Galina Barskaya: 55 top right. Tony Campbell: 21 top, 34 top. Phil Date: 24 top right (CD). Frenc: 20 left, 29 bottom right. Marianna Raszkowska: 29 top right. Kristian Sekulic: 5 bottom right. Eti Swinford: 28 bottom center. Marzanna Syncerz: 57 top right. Iana Turnaeva: 24 top left.

Fotolia.com:
Callalloo Twisty: 26 bottom. Tony Campbell: 1, 15, 16 center left, 17 top right, 17 center, 25 bottom. Willee Cole: Back cover center right, 50 top center, 59 top right. Digital_Zombie: 42 bottom right. Zoran Djekic: Back cover top right, 39 top right. Rafael Goetter: 36 center. Jeanne Hatch: 30 bottom. Petar Ishmeriev: 35 top right. Kavita: 37 center left. Natalia Lisovskaya: 14 top and center. Perrush: 41 top. Dalia Rukiene: 51 bottom left. Kristian Sekulic: 17 bottom right.

Maksim Shmeljov: 36 top center. Oleksandr Slyadnyev: 35 bottom. Carolina K Smith MD: 47 top right. Tom Stewart: 48 center right. Tatarszkij: 38 bottom right. Zzzdim: 31 bottom right.

Interpet Archive: 22 top left (guinea pigs), 32 inset, 33 center right, 36 bottom, 51 center left, 56 top left, 59 top center.

iStockphoto.com:
Gary Alvis: 37 top right. Mariya Bibikova: 11 bottom right, 56 bottom. Tony Campbell: Cover front flap, 58 top right. Rhienna Cutler: 45 bottom. Simon Denson: 21 (lily). Claudia Dewald: 20 top right. Wendell Franks: 21 (holly). David Gilder: 26 top right. Eric Isselée: 52 top. Stefan Klein: 16 bottom right. Mitja Mladkovic: 39 bottom. Rafal Olkis: 30 top left. Michael Pettigrew: 25 top right. Jillian Pond: 38 left. Lesa Sweet: 27 center left. Willie B. Thomas: 23 bottom left, 49 bottom left. Beverley Vycital: 54 bottom right.

Shutterstock Inc.:
Tony Campbell: 16 top right, 22 top left (kitten). Ekaterina Cherkashina: 52 bottom left. Lars Christensen: 18 bottom, 54 bottom left. Anna Dzondzua: 54 top. Stephen Finn: 52 center right. Jeanne Hatch: Cover (front inset). Ingret: 26 top left. Julie Keen: 50 top left. Ariusz Nawrocki: Front cover main image. Tina Rencelj: 19 top right. Robynrg: 41 bottom right. Vladimir Mihajlovich Suponev: 9. Ustyujanin: 53. Yellowj: 51 top left.

Hardback case: Interpet Publishing Archive (front cover center right), Dreamstime.com/Tony Campbell (back cover top right), iStock.com/Tony Campbell (front cover center left), iStock.com/Tony Campbell/Rafal Zdeb (front cover top montage), Shutterstock.com/Tony Campbell (spine), Warren Photographic (back cover top left and bottom, inside endpaper).